Introduction to

You've Already Got It!

Andrew Wommack

© Copyright 2023 – Andrew Wommack

Printed in the United States of America. All rights reserved. No portion of this book may be reproduced, stored in a retrieval system, or transmitted in any form or by any means—electronic, mechanical, photocopy, recording, scanning, or other—except for brief quotations in critical reviews or articles, without the prior written permission of the publisher.

Unless otherwise indicated, all Scripture quotations are taken from the King James Version® of the Bible. Copyright © by the British Crown. Public domain.

All emphasis within Scripture quotations is the author's own.

Published in partnership between Andrew Wommack Ministries and Harrison House Publishers.

Woodland Park, CO 80863 – Shippensburg, PA 17257

ISBN 13 TP: 978-1-59548-614-1

For Worldwide Distribution, Printed in the USA

1 2 3 4 5 6 / 26 25 24 23

Contents

Introduction	1
Fight the Good Fight	3
We Are Not Desperate	6
Don't Ask for What You Already Have	9
Benefits of the Atonement	13
Don't Settle for Less	16
Grace Makes Available	19
Faith Appropriates	22
Labor to Enter into Rest	25
Acknowledge Every Good Thing	28
Superior Position and Power	31
Believe It's Done	35
Don't Blame God	39
Just Believe God	42
I Got It!	44
Conclusion	48
Receive Jesus as Your Savior	51
Receive the Holy Spirit	53

Introduction

Do you struggle to believe God for things like healing or financial blessing? Are you frustrated by trying to get things from God? Well, the problem isn't with God. He's already provided everything!

You don't need to ask God to heal you, bless you, prosper you, or reveal His love to you. He's already done all these things. What you've got to do is learn how to start receiving instead of asking God to start giving. That's a paradigm shift!

If you could understand how important this is, you would see much better results in your life. That's what happened to me once I got the mindset that God has already done His part. It's not up to me to beg and plead with God to do something. I just need to draw out what God has already put in me instead of asking God to give me things.

I have ministered for over fifty years, teaching about how God already loves you, He's already blessed you (Eph. 1:3), and that you already have all things in heavenly places in Christ. After I teach in my meetings, I have people come up and ask, "Would you please pray that God would give me His love?" or "Would you please pray that God would heal me?" Those kinds of prayers go against everything I teach.

Realizing I already have access to all of God's blessings is one of the most important things He has ever shown me, but it had to come by revelation. There is no natural way to understand something that you cannot see—that you can't prove in some physical way. You've got to receive this through the revelation of the Holy Spirit. The good news is that God wants to reveal this to you more than you want Him to reveal it, and this booklet will explain how!

Fight the Good Fight

Not long after I got turned on to the Lord, March 23, 1968, I was drafted into the Army and sent to

Vietnam. I took my Bible with me, and I studied the Word up to fifteen hours a day for thirteen months. I had every page marked up. Within a few years, nearly my entire Bible was taped together because it was so well used. Pages had fallen out, and entire books were missing. By the time I was pastoring my first little church in Seagoville, Texas, I didn't even have a whole Bible to preach from. I just needed a new one.

We were living in poverty then, which wasn't God's fault. It was my fault. Jamie and I would go weeks at a time without eating, and our situation was critical. Now, maybe you can't relate to this because when you say you are broke, maybe you've got $1,000 in the bank but $2,000 worth of bills to pay. Still, you've got money. When I say that Jamie and I were broke, I mean we didn't have anything—not even pocket change. I'd even pick up and redeem glass bottles for gas money!

Finally, I made the decision that I needed to start seeing what I was preaching about—healing, deliverance, provision, and other things—come to pass. It couldn't just be talk. I had to have some proof of it. So, I just focused on one thing. I said, "I'm going to buy myself a new Bible."

I drew a line in the sand and said, "I'm going to live or die right here. Either faith works and I'm going to see it produce a new Bible, or I'm just going to quit." What good was I going to be in ministry if I couldn't even believe for a new Bible? How can I help anybody else get born again, healed, delivered, and prosperous if I couldn't even believe for enough money to get the book that has those truths in it?

> **There is a struggle in the Christian life, but it isn't with God to get something from Him.**

I knew God wanted me to make disciples (Matt. 28:19–20), so I could trust He would also provide the Bible to do it (Phil. 4:19). In that moment, I decided to put a stake in the ground and fight the good fight of faith according to 1 Timothy 6:12:

Fight the good fight of faith, lay hold on eternal life, whereunto thou art also called, and hast professed a good profession before many witnesses.

The Greek word that was translated "fight" in this verse is *agōnizomai*,[1] and it means "to struggle, … to compete for a prize, … to contend with an adversary, or … to endeavor to accomplish something." It comes from the same root word that we get the English words *agony* and *agonize* from.

There is a struggle in the Christian life, but it isn't with God to get something from Him. We fight against our own thoughts and the devil's lies that we need something more than what God has already provided. We need to get to a place where we say, "This is non-negotiable. If God tells me to do something, He's already provided everything I need to get the job done. I'll stand here and do it." We need to fight a good fight against the enemy—and a good fight is one you win!

We Are Not Desperate

A popular song that's been sung in many church worship services over the years—called "This Is the Air I Breathe"—encourages people to declare how desperate they are for God's presence and how lost they are without Him. It says God's presence is the air we breathe, and His Word is our daily bread.[2]

Now, I like the music in the song, and I've sung along with it, but I change some of the words because *I am not desperate for God.* I agree that we should be as dependent upon God's presence as we are upon our breath. We should be as dependent upon God's Word as we are the food that we eat. I agree with a lot of what the song says and I'm not condemning anyone. But that phrase, "I'm desperate for you," is not something believers should be singing.

Webster's 1828 Dictionary, which helps people better understand words in the *King James Version* of the Bible, defines *desperate*[3] five ways. One of the definitions is "without hope." I can guarantee you I am not without hope. Now, I would be without hope if I was without God, but I'm not without God. I don't think a Christian ought to be without hope.

The second definition means, "without care of safety; rash; fearless of danger." When a person is desperate, they do desperate things. As believers, we shouldn't be under so much pressure that we are going to do something illogical and irrational because we are desperate to get something from God. That's not a good way to describe a Christian.

> What's inside your born-again spirit is more important than outside circumstances.

The third definition is "furious, as a man in despair." The apostle Paul wrote,

But we have this treasure in earthen vessels, that the excellency of the power may be of God, and not of us. We are troubled on every side, yet not distressed; we are perplexed, but

***not in despair**; persecuted, but not forsaken; cast down, but not destroyed.*

2 Corinthians 4:7–9

Paul said there were times he had trouble, but it didn't distress him. He was perplexed, but he didn't despair. He was persecuted but never forsaken. He was cast down but never destroyed. As a believer, what's inside your born-again spirit is more important than outside circumstances. Acting out of despair is not part of the Christian life.

The fourth definition is "hopeless; despaired of; lost beyond hope of recovery; irretrievable, irrecoverable; forlorn." Sad to say, I believe this describes the majority of people who sing about being desperate for God. It's because they don't understand the truth that He's already provided everything they need.

People are seeking healing, prosperity, joy, and peace with an attitude of hopelessness and despair. And when they sing this song, it's giving in to these feelings of frustration. They are thinking, *Oh God,*

I'm sick, I'm poor, I'm stressed out, and I'm in fear. They are feeling hopeless; just begging God to do something. I'll tell you, that is not a godly attitude.

Don't Ask for What You Already Have

I remember ministering at a church where the people had just sung that song about being desperate for God and lost without Him. Now, instead of just amplifying a negative situation, I typically just change the words so I can sing, "God, I'm *in love with* you, and I *won't* live without you." But, in this case, I felt like people were using *desperate* and *lost* in the worst sense of the words. They were just singing Christian blues and amplifying their hurts and pains.

Then, they got me in a back room and prayed over me, "Oh God, we ask You to anoint Andrew today. We ask You to flow through Andrew." I hear these things a lot at churches. They nearly always want to pray over me and ask God to anoint me. When they do that, I think to myself, *If you don't believe I'm anointed, and you've got to ask God just five minutes before I go out there to anoint me and give me something to say, then why did you even ask me to come?* That has an element of unbelief in it.

See, this isn't how I live my life. I don't pray, "Oh God, please touch and anoint me." When God called me to minister, He would've been unjust to call me to preach His Word and not anoint me to do it. Anything that God calls you to do, you are already anointed to do it. It's not a matter of asking God to do it. It's a matter of believing that He has done it, then appropriate it, and walk in it by faith.

> Anything that God calls you to do, you are already anointed to do it.

What's more, people pray, begging God to come to church, saying, "Oh God, we ask You to come and be with us today." And as they leave the service, they pray, "Oh God, go with us throughout this week and bless us." Those are not effective prayers!

People pray like that because, if they don't see it or feel it, they don't believe what God promised. They feel like they have to petition God for everything. There are many times in church services that if nobody jumps a pew, shouts, gets healed, or anything else visible happens, people will say, "God wasn't within a hundred miles of that place." What they're doing is expressing how they feel. God was already there, but they just didn't experience Him with their physical senses.

The Bible says God will never leave you nor forsake you (Heb. 13:5). Why would you ask God to go with you if He said, *"I'll never leave [you], nor forsake [you]"*? Jesus also said,

> *For where two or three are gathered together in my name, there am I in the midst of them.*
>
> Matthew 18:20

After this church finished singing about being desperate and hungry for God, and praying for the

Lord's anointing to be on the service, I got up and asked, "How many of you are desperate for God?" And a lot of them including the pastor started shouting and screaming. So, I started showing them Hebrews 13:5 and Matthew 18:20. I also told them that believers will never hunger (John 6:34–35) or thirst (John 4:13–14).

After I shared that, it got so quiet, you could have heard a pin drop. I'm not sure that's the way I should've done it, but Jesus said that if you came to Him, you should never be hungry or thirsty again. As believers, we shouldn't be desperate.

People who are desperate for God are in unbelief. They are constantly asking God to move or do something new. They think He is withholding something from them, so that's why they beg and plead for Him to do something. That is just wrong!

Benefits of the Atonement

> *Therefore if any man* be *in Christ,* he is *a new creature: old things are passed away; behold,*

all things are become new. For [God] hath made [Jesus] to be *sin for us, who knew no sin; that we might be made the righteousness of God in him.*

2 Corinthians 5:17, 21

There are many of you who don't have confidence God will bless you unless you do something religious to make Him give it to you. But that way of thinking will actually keep you from receiving what God has already provided through the atonement of Jesus.

Every sin, sickness, and disease of the entire human race—every deformity, tumor, and perversion—entered into the physical body of the Lord Jesus Christ. That's why His face looked worse than any other person who has ever lived, and His form became so distorted that He didn't even look human. He became sin so we could become the righteousness of God (2 Cor. 5:21). That's the atonement.

Modern-day Christianity has divided what Jesus did through the atonement into different parts, saying that forgiveness of sins is the only thing that applies to every person (1 John 2:2). They say that everything else is conditional, and God may or may not bless you, heal you, financially prosper you, or give you joy and peace. Many people look at all those things as optional, but the Bible doesn't make that distinction.

The Greek word σῴζω (*"sōzō"*), often translated "save," is also translated "made whole."[4] This is the New Testament's all-inclusive word for what Jesus accomplished through the atonement. It applies to forgiveness of sins, healing, deliverance, prosperity, and everything else Jesus made available to us by taking the sins of the whole world into His own body on the cross.

Let's take healing for example:

[Jesus] bare our sins in his own body on the tree, that we, being dead to sins, should live unto righteousness: by whose stripes ye were healed.

1 Peter 2:24

If you recognize that healing is part of the atonement, then you'd understand that the Lord has already healed us. If you *were* healed, that means you *are* healed. He's already purchased that blessing, and that power has already been generated. The same thing applies to prosperity, deliverance, or anything else we need.

> If you *were* healed, that means you *are* healed.

The woman suffering from the issue of blood who touched the hem of Jesus' garment in the crowd was not only sick, but she also *"had spent all her living upon physicians, neither could be healed of any"* (Luke 8:43). After power flowed out from Jesus and into her body, He ministered to the woman:

> *And he said unto her, Daughter, be of good comfort: thy faith hath made thee whole; go in peace.*
>
> Luke 8:48

The word *"sōzō"* was used in that verse for *whole*. Now, we know this woman was healed, but when you put the verse back in its context, you can see the power to be restored financially was also available to her. We don't know if she received it, but it was there. You've got to get to a place where you can see *everything* from God is already yours if you're willing to receive it.

Don't Settle for Less

For I know the thoughts that I think toward you, saith the Lord, *thoughts of peace, and not of evil, to give you an expected end.*

Jeremiah 29:11

One of the reasons we don't receive everything God has for us is because we are willing to settle for less. We have been influenced more by the world than by God's Word and conditioned to accept far less than what God has provided. As long as you can live with less of God, you will. That is a powerful truth!

You have to get sick and tired of being sick and tired before you will receive from God. You need to have a holy dissatisfaction with mediocrity before you can experience all God has for you. It doesn't happen accidentally or automatically, though. You have to seek God through His Word and in prayer.

When the Lord spoke to the prophet Jeremiah, Israel was devastated. Jerusalem had been destroyed, and many people were taken to Babylon in captivity. Thoughts of peace were probably the last thing on their minds, but Jeremiah went on to say in verses 11–13:

For I know the thoughts that I think toward you, saith the LORD, thoughts of peace, and not of evil, to give you an expected end. Then shall ye call upon me, and ye shall go and pray unto me, and I will hearken unto you. And ye shall seek me, and find me, *when ye shall search for me with all your heart.*

I've had people tell me they prayed and believed God, but then nothing happened. But the key is to seek God, not just the thing we are believing for. I'll tell you, all the good things God has done in my life and ministry have come out of my relationship with Him because I seek and know Him intimately. I know He has the best for me—an expected end.

It reminds me of the time a man came forward for prayer in one of my meetings. He told me he had a terrible pain in his neck and couldn't sleep. He continued, "I've got a back problem; my sciatic nerve causes pain down my entire leg and into my foot; I have neuropathy," and on and on he went. Then he said, "But if God could just heal the pain in my neck, I could live with the rest."

I looked at him and said, "Well, I understand. If we asked God to heal all of those things at once, the lights in heaven might dim. I'm not sure God could pull that off." That guy just looked at me for a minute, and then he replied, "That was pretty stupid, wasn't it?" I agreed and then went on to tell him that he didn't have to just settle—that the Lord had already made healing available for his whole body.

The truth is, we may not know God as we should, but it's not His fault. The Lord said, *"My people are destroyed for lack of knowledge"* (Hos. 4:6). Specifically, the knowledge about the very nature and character of God is missing in many Christians' lives. That's why they beg and try to twist God's arm to get something. If they would just seek Him and study His Word, they would find that He loves them, and that everything good is already provided.

Grace Makes Available

Blessed be *the God and Father of our Lord Jesus Christ, who hath blessed us with all spiritual blessings in heavenly* places *in Christ.*

Ephesians 1:3

The book of Ephesians is written from the perspective of everything already being ours in Christ. When Jesus cried, *"It is finished"* (John 19:30), He meant just that. His work on earth was done. The atonement was complete. He provided everything we could ever need, and that's grace!

By definition, the word *grace* means "the free unmerited love and favor of God."[5] Another way of saying it is, grace is God's part. We aren't waiting on Him to give; He is waiting on us to receive!

Any blessing you could ever need or desire from the Lord is not something to strive for but something you already have. God made the provision before you had the need. It is just a simple matter of receiving what He has already done. The benefit of understanding and being assured of this is enormous. It kills legalism and the performance mentality, and that will take a huge load off you. How could you doubt that God will give you something if He has already given it to you?

You are probably thinking, *Well, that's great! But if I already have it, where is it?* It's in the spiritual realm and, more specifically, your born-again spirit. God has deposited everything you need on the inside of you, and you can draw those things out by sowing the incorruptible seed of God's Word (1 Pet. 1:23).

For example, we struggled financially for years until I started meditating on about a hundred scriptures regarding prosperity. It was like a dam broke, and everything the Lord had been trying to flow through me suddenly came forth. Our ministry is growing like never before, but those things were actually inside my born-again spirit the entire time.

Many people just can't grasp this truth because they are trapped in their five senses. If they can't see, taste, smell, touch, or hear it, they don't think it exists. Therefore, when you say they have already been healed, they check their physical bodies with their five senses, and if they don't look or feel healed, they say they aren't.

The same applies to prosperity. If you tell someone, "*My God shall supply all your need according to his riches in glory by Christ Jesus*" (Phil. 4:19), but they look at their bank account and don't see enough money to pay their bills, they may not believe it. That's because they aren't seeing it in the spiritual realm, based on what God's Word says.

You see, God moves in the spiritual realm. Whether or not we see something manifest in the physical realm, what He has already done in the spiritual realm is no longer dependent on His giving but on our receiving. We have to know that God has already done His part—providing everything we need through the atonement—and that any delay in the manifestation is not His fault. It may be our fault, the devil's fault, or someone else's fault, but it's never God's fault.

Faith Appropriates

Faith is not what you do to get a response from God, but faith is simply your positive response to what God has already done by grace. In other words, you appropriate what God has already made available through grace by using your faith. If God hasn't already provided something by grace, your faith can't get it. It can't make Him move.

Grace and faith work together, and they must be in balance. Think of it this way: grace is what

God does; faith is what we do. It takes both working together.

> *For by grace are ye saved through faith; and that not of yourselves:* it is *the gift of God: not of works, lest any man should boast.*
>
> Ephesians 2:8–9

God's grace has provided for every need in your life. That provision is not based on whether you are reading the Bible enough, praying enough, going to church every time the doors are open, or even paying your tithes. Before you ever had a financial need, God created the provision (Phil. 4:19). Before you were sick, God provided your healing (1 Pet. 2:24). Before you ever became discouraged, God blessed you with all spiritual blessings (Eph. 1:3). God anticipated every need you could ever have and has met those needs through Jesus before you existed.

Many Christians believe that God moves sovereignly *as* He wills *when* He wills. That's because religion teaches that God controls everything and that nothing can happen without His permission. However, it's not true—everything isn't up to God. I believe the "sovereignty of God teaching" is the worst doctrine in the church today; it's a real faith killer.

When people don't receive by faith what God has provided through grace, they just blame God. They believe God is withholding His blessings because of some sovereign plan, and they are just waiting on Him to move. But Jesus hasn't saved, healed, delivered, or prospered a single person in the last 2,000 years. What God provided by grace 2,000 years ago becomes a reality when mixed with faith. Faith appropriates (assigns for a particular purpose) what God has already provided.

> God anticipated every need you could ever have and has met those needs through Jesus before you existed.

God isn't withholding something from you, and faith doesn't make God do anything. Grace and faith have to work together, and our part is to accept what God has already done.

Labor to Enter into Rest

There remaineth therefore a rest to the people of God. For he that is entered into his rest, he also hath ceased from his own works, as God did from his. Let us labour therefore to enter into that rest, lest any man fall after the same example of unbelief.

Hebrews 4:9–11

Faith is really just resting and trusting in God—but it takes work to rest! It's not easy to sit there when your body is screaming at you that you're dying, when your bank account says you don't have the money, when relationships are falling apart, and everything's going bad. It takes effort to rest in what God has said.

Maybe you've felt frustrated or burned out from

constantly trying to believe God in the face of circumstances. Well, you're not alone. It's been said that four out of five ministers quit ministry within the first five years.[6] Dr. James Dobson (founder of Focus on the Family) even reported that 80 percent of ministers still pursuing their callings suffer from discouragement or depression.[7] That means that only a very small percentage of people are not ministering out of burnout. And these are the people who are supposed to train up the body of Christ for the work of the ministry (Eph. 4:11–13)! That's just terrible!

Really, a person who's burned out is just doing things out of their own strength; they are doing things just to get God to respond to them. Most people think they have to work to earn the blessings of God instead of receiving what is available through what Jesus has already done—through grace. They think, *I have to read the Bible every day, I have to go to church, I have to pay my tithes, I have to live holy*, and on and on it goes. It's like if they put a coin in a slot machine and pull the handle, God's blessings will come out.

You just have to get to the place where you say, "God, you've already done it. Whatever you've called me to do, you've already given me the anointing that it takes to do it. You've already provided everything. Before I had the need, the supply was already there."

I'm here to tell you that your actions don't make God do anything; it's faith that just reaches out and appropriates what He has already done. It's true that you need to go to church, study the Word, and give. But if you think God owes you something because you do all those things, then you have moved out of faith and into legalism. That will actually stop the power of God from flowing in your life.

> God is waiting on you to believe what His Word says.

You've got to spend time in the Word, seek God, and pray. But as you do these things, you rest in what Christ has already done for you, not what you are doing for Him. That takes all the struggle out of your spiritual walk and eliminates the risk of burnout. Draw upon your relationship with God, and rest in Him.

Acknowledge Every Good Thing

That the communication of thy faith may become effectual by the acknowledging of every good thing which is in you in Christ Jesus.

Philemon 1:6

When Paul was praying for Philemon, he prayed that the *"communication of thy faith may become effectual."* That means it would begin to work, *"by the acknowledging of every good thing which is in you in Christ Jesus."* Now, you can't acknowledge something that doesn't already exist. The word *acknowledge* just means "to admit the existence or truth of" something.[8]

In other words, the way Paul was praying for Philemon wasn't by saying, "Oh God, touch him," or "Oh God, do something new in him." But he was saying, "God, help him to recognize and acknowledge what You've already done." And the truth is, there are people who need to be healed in their bodies, need a financial blessing, or need their marriages restored; but in all of those things, God has already done His part.

You aren't waiting on God to answer your prayer. God is waiting on you to believe what His Word says—that He's already done it. When Jesus hung on the cross, He said, *"It is finished"* (John 19:30). He has already done everything, and now He is seated at the Father's right hand (Heb. 10:12).

Born-again believers who experience the power of the Lord flowing through them and manifesting in their lives have learned that God has already done His part. He has delivered power and authority to them, and they release the healing power, the delivering power, the prosperity power, and the relational power God put on the inside of them. Letting the Lord flow through them enables them to walk in victory.

Sad to say, there are millions of Christians who believe God *can* do anything, but they don't believe

He *has* done anything. They just believe He could do it, and they are in the process of begging God and asking Him to do something. They won't believe God has done anything until they can see it. They won't believe in a healing until they can go to a doctor and prove it. Or they won't believe in a financial blessing until they can go to the bank and withdraw the money.

The truth is that God has already done His part, and we've got to believe it. He's put power on the inside of us, and it's just a matter of us releasing what He has done instead of trying to get Him to do something new.

The Lord has already given you everything that you will ever need (2 Pet. 1:3). You don't need anything else, so it's not a matter of just getting God to do something. It's a matter of learning what He's already done, how to release it, and how to take your authority and command that power to flow through you.

Superior Position and Power

But God, who is rich in mercy, for his great love wherewith he loved us, even when we were dead in sins, hath quickened us together with Christ, (by grace ye are saved;) and hath raised *us up together, and made* us *sit together in heavenly* places *in Christ Jesus.*

Ephesians 2:4–6

It is so much different to believe that God has already done something than to believe He could do something but hasn't done it yet. For instance, He has already raised us up in the spiritual realm and made us sit together with Jesus. We're not waiting for God to raise us up spiritually because He's already done it. That's awesome!

In the same way we are on the spiritual high ground with Jesus, soldiers who fight from an elevated position have a strategic advantage.

When I was in the military in Vietnam, I was stationed on a small fire-support base about forty miles from the nearest U.S. military installation. We would have a machine gun placed on top of a hill, and five people in that position could hold off a hundred others attacking them. We provided artillery support to soldiers patrolling beyond the range of their base camps and were in an elevated position that was easily defensible.

Nothing would happen on that support base for a long time, but suddenly we would come under attack, Five thousand North Vietnamese troops surrounded our mountaintop where only 120 American soldiers were stationed. That would put us on "red alert," meaning all troops were supposed to stay awake all night and be on bunker guard together instead of taking turns the way they normally did.

Just after I arrived on the fire support base, I had bunker guard duty one night all by myself. The other soldiers assigned to that bunker just fell asleep. The next night, I was too tired to do it by myself again, so I asked that they stay up and help me. One of the other soldiers said, "You must be new here." When I responded that I was, the others laughed. Then they told me how superior our firepower was compared to what the enemy had. If they ever came out of their holes, we would wipe them out in minutes. They described to me all the different weapons we had and how powerful they were.

During a red alert, an American combat helicopter also circled overhead throughout the night. Just one fifty-caliber mini-gun on that helicopter could spray an area the size of a football field with rounds spaced every six inches. Just the concussion from a fifty-caliber bullet can kill a person if it comes within six inches of their head! The vast superiority of our weapons overwhelmed me. And, in a short period of time, I fell asleep with the others.

I ended up spending my twenty-first birthday in Vietnam, and it was one of those days we came under attack. But this time, we took multiple direct hits on the bunker I was in. We could see the muzzle fire from our enemies' weapons. On nights like that, I can guarantee you, nobody was sleeping on bunker duty. We knew they were out there trying to kill us, but it still would have required far more of them to overtake our position than we needed to defend it. We just needed to draw on our superior firepower to overcome the attack.

The lies of the enemy may try to get you to believe you need to get something more from God, but they are not nearly as powerful as the truths in the Word of God, which says we already have everything we need. The devil is trying to make us see that we are grasshoppers in our own sight (Num. 13:33) rather than believe we are seated in heavenly places in Christ (Eph. 2:6). We're not supposed to be fighting to take the higher ground because we are already there. We are not fighting *for* victory, but instead we are fighting *from* victory. Amen!

Believe It's Done

Therefor I say unto you, What things so ever ye desire, when ye pray, believe that ye receive them, *and ye shall have* them.

Mark 11:24

If you can understand these things, it will make a difference in the way you receive from God. If the manifestation doesn't come right away when you pray for healing, don't say, "God, I don't know why You haven't healed me yet. But I'm asking You to move!" You don't have to start fasting and recruiting other people to bombard heaven with prayers, plead with God, and make Him heal you. That whole mindset is unbelief. You didn't actually believe that you received when you prayed.

> We're not supposed to be fighting to take the higher ground because we are already there.

You must believe you receive the *very instant* you pray, not when you see it later. You may be thinking, *How can I believe God answered my prayer if I don't feel healed right away?* You see, the moment you prayed, it was already a done deal in the spirit. Your answer is already a reality in the spiritual world.

Now, another thing to consider is that whatever you're believing for is not going to manifest by itself. God works through people. And because He works through people, their participation in your miracle is dependent on their own obedience.

In Acts 9:10–12, God called Ananias to minister healing to Saul of Tarsus (later, the apostle Paul). But when the Lord spoke to him in a vision, Ananias responded,

> *Lord, I have heard by many of this man, how much evil he hath done to thy saints at Jerusalem: and here he hath authority from the chief priests to bind all that call on thy name.*

Acts 9:13b–14

God wanted to heal Saul, but His will wasn't going to come to pass automatically. Ananias had to be obedient. After the Lord explained His plans for Saul's life, Ananias went and entered into the house to minister healing (vv. 15–17). Praise God that Ananias was obedient. What if he hadn't been willing to wait on the Lord? Would there have been someone else who carried out God's will? Many times, God's will doesn't come to pass because people aren't obedient.

Another way people don't receive what God already has for them is because of demonic resistance. A friend of mine had his house up for sale "by owner." He'd put a sign in his yard but had been unable to sell it for two years. The market wasn't good, and few people had actually looked at the house.

He heard me teach these things, and the Lord spoke to him, saying, "I moved on someone to buy your house the very first day you put it up for sale, but Satan has been hindering them." It wasn't this man's fault, but demonic opposition had been hindering the manifestation of his blessing. Since my friend didn't know what the situation was, he prayed over it in tongues, believing that God was interceding through him (Rom. 8:26). Two days later, his house sold.

While they were going through the closing, the man buying the house told my friend, "The very first day you put that sign in your yard, I told my wife, 'That's our house!' I've been trying for two years now to get my finances together, but I haven't been able to. Then the strangest thing happened. Two days ago, the man who'd been trying to buy my house came over with cash, and we closed. It's taken me a day or so to get things together so I could come over here and do this. But here I am!"

God had made available the blessing two years before, but the holdup wasn't the Lord. It was Satan who had hindered other people. God has *"blessed us with all spiritual blessings in heavenly places in Christ"* (Eph. 1:3). It's already done. He's commanded these blessings upon you, but they are in the spiritual realm. By faith, you must bring things out of the spirit and into the physical realm, but it requires people's obedience and overcoming demonic resistance.

Don't Blame God

Everything that happens in this world isn't just up to God. He doesn't just sovereignly move. God operates through people, which means you have a part to play in somebody else's miracle. He's already provided the blessing before the need, but we have to cooperate and use our faith to appropriate His grace. And when things go wrong, it's not God's fault because He's already done His part.

Years ago, a couple in our church had a child with severe birth defects. The mother was a very small woman, and she delivered this baby boy in a taxi on the way to the hospital. It caused him to have brain damage, and because of birth defects, his immune system was deficient. The doctor said that if the child ever got a cold, he would die; there was nothing they could do for him. They didn't expect him to live very long, but when I met this family, the boy was already four years old.

Eventually, he did get a cold. So, I went to their house and prayed over him to be healed. While holding the child in my arms, he died. We sat there for hours with the parents and prayed for this little boy to be raised from the dead. We did everything I knew to do, but he didn't revive. It was a very tragic situation.

The parents asked me to minister at his funeral. They were grieving, and it would have been comforting to come up with some of the clichés that you hear commonly given in religion: "God works in mysterious ways," "He must have wanted your son in heaven," or "God needed him there." But I had to be honest with the Word.

I remembered when my father died when I was twelve years old, and I was told God needed him in heaven more than I needed him here. Even as a young boy, I knew better than that. Why would God need my dad in heaven? God didn't kill my dad. That is not what the Word of God teaches. The Scripture makes it very clear that Jesus came to destroy the works of the devil (Heb. 2:14 and 1 John 3:8). Satan is the one who goes about seeking whom he may devour (1 Pet. 5:8). The devil is the one who comes to steal, kill, and destroy (John 10:10).

I told those parents, "I don't believe this was God's will. The Lord did not kill your son. He didn't allow this to happen. Satan was the one who snuffed out his life. Even though the devil may have won this battle, he didn't win the war." Then I shared from 2 Samuel 12:23 and other scriptures how this child was now in the presence of God. I ministered hope, and the reality that this boy was with Jesus.

It may have been comforting momentarily to the parents to have just said, "Well, it couldn't have been us that missed it. We gave it everything we had." But when it came to why it happened, I basically said, "It's either my fault, your fault, both of our faults, or things that we don't understand. I don't know what it is, but I can guarantee you, it's not God."

Just Believe God

The doctors had told this woman the reason her child had birth defects was because she was so small. They said that if she ever got pregnant again, the baby would have to be delivered by C-section, and that both she and the child would probably lose their lives anyway. So, they advised her to never have children again.

In contrast, because I told these people the truth after their son died, they prayed, and God showed them some areas where they had allowed fear, doubt, and unbelief to come in. These things had hindered their faith and kept them from receiving the miracle they needed. Because they received the truth, they repented and were able to overcome those fears.

That woman ended up giving birth to multiple children after her son died. She had all-natural childbirths at home without any doctors because she knew that no one, after seeing her medical records, would agree to help her have another baby. So, she just believed God. She eventually sent me a picture of all her kids. They graduated high school and went on to college. That's awesome!

> It's not God who fails to heal people; we are the ones who fail to receive.

Instead of going childless and living her entire life in bitterness, wondering why God didn't heal her son, she was able to go on and have other children because she took hold of the truth, and the truth set her free (John 8:32). Instead of agreeing with the doctors or somehow rationalizing their diagnosis by believing God didn't want her to have more children, she trusted in the Word.

Children are a gift from God (Ps. 127:3). Before God forms children in the womb, He knows them (Jer. 1:5). The Lord covers babies in their mothers' wombs, and fearfully and wonderfully makes them

(Ps. 139:13–16). All the children this family had were known to God first, and He had plans for them. He made available a way for them to be born healthy and strong so they could fulfill those plans. They just needed their mother and father to believe God, not blame Him for their failure, and be faithful to the grace He provided. Amen!

I understand why people would want to say that boy's death must have been "God's will," but it's an easy way out. It's not God who fails to heal people; we are the ones who fail to receive. We have to believe and cooperate with God to receive what He has already provided for us.

I Got It!

Let's go back to when I was believing for a new Bible as a young pastor in Seagoville, Texas. When I decided to believe God for enough money to buy one, it took me nearly six months to come up with an extra $25 so I could. Again, some of you can't relate to that, but I'm saying that's how poor we were. We were so poor we couldn't pay attention. We were struggling.

During those six months, there was probably not any waking moment that I didn't have some fear or worry about whether or not it was going to work. The devil knew how important this was to me, and he fought me tooth and toenail. I had the enemy condemning me with thoughts like, *What kind of a man of God are you? You don't even have a whole Bible!* Eventually, I got that $25 and bought that new Bible. I even had my name engraved on it. And when I walked out of that bookstore and had that Bible under my arm, I never doubted again that I would get what I believed for.

I know some of you are thinking, *Well, of course. Why would you doubt that you're going to get it if you've already got it?* That's my point! God had already provided for a new Bible, but I had to appropriate it by my faith. I had to believe that Bible was mine, even before it was in my hand.

It didn't really take six months for me to get a Bible. It just took six months for me to believe it and withstand the enemy's lies that were driving my unbelief. Once I had it in my hands, there was no room for doubt, but there was really no reason to doubt at all. I already had it in the spirit realm, and it was just a matter of time before it manifested in the physical!

You might say, "I believe I'm healed," but you don't *really* believe you are healed. You may believe you are *going* to be healed, and because of it, you're doubting. That's because you don't view healing as something that has already been done but as something that has yet to be accomplished. You pray, but you think God isn't responding—He's silent.

In my meetings, I'll sometimes walk over to someone and hand them my Bible. Then I ask, "Now, what would I do if you asked me for my Bible? How do you think I would respond?" In reality, I'd probably just stare at them and be totally quiet, wondering why they would be asking for something they already have. Many Christians, when they pray for what they've already got, are getting total silence from the Lord. It's because God has already given them everything they need.

If God could be confused, I think He would be confused. He might say, "I told them in My Word that they were already blessed, healed, prosperous, and had total joy and peace in their spirits. Why are they asking Me for what they already have? Why do they ask Me to come into their services when I said I would always be in the midst of two or three of them? Why do they ask Me to go with them when I said I would never leave them or forsake them?"

If you could just see that you've already got it—that you've already got on the inside of you the same power that raised Christ from the dead (Eph. 1:18–20), you would quit dealing with doubt. You just need to see what God has done as an accomplished fact instead of something that could happen in the future.

Conclusion

Do you need to be saved? It says in 1 John 2:2 that Jesus *"is the propitiation for our sins: and not for ours only, but also for* the sins of *the whole world."* He's already forgiven the sins of the entire world. It's not a matter of whether God will forgive you; He's already forgiven sins. The question is, Will you receive His forgiveness? Will you put faith in what Jesus has already done? That's the real issue.

In the same way God has already forgiven you, He's already healed you, He's already commanded His blessing upon you and your finances, and He's already given you love, joy, and peace. You don't need God to respond to you; you need to learn to respond to God! It's easier to stand on something you already have than to go get something you don't have.

That is so powerful, but this is where so many Christians are missing it. They know that God *can* do all these things, but they don't believe He's done anything yet. They start from a position of unbelief.

They are crossways with the Word of God. But they don't have to stay that way, and neither do you!

I hope this booklet has given you some insight from the Word of God. I hope that now you will see that you already have everything you need to be successful in this life, and it's only a matter of appropriating the things God's provided. You've already got it, so quit trying to get it!

FURTHER STUDY

If you enjoyed this booklet and would like to learn more about some of the things I've shared, I suggest my teachings:

1. *Plain as Dirt*
2. *A Better Way to Pray*
3. *God Wants You Well*
4. *Living in the Balance of Grace and Faith*
5. *Financial Stewardship*
6. *You've Already Got It!*

These teachings are available for free at **awmi.net**, or they can be purchased at **awmi.net/store**.

Receive Jesus as Your Savior

Choosing to receive Jesus Christ as your Lord and Savior is the most important decision you'll ever make!

God's Word promises, *"That if thou shalt confess with thy mouth the Lord Jesus, and shalt believe in thine heart that God hath raised him from the dead, thou shalt be saved. For with the heart man believeth unto righteousness; and with the mouth confession is made unto salvation"* (Rom. 10:9–10). *"For whosoever shall call upon the name of the Lord shall be saved"* (Rom. 10:13). By His grace, God has already done everything to provide salvation. Your part is simply to believe and receive.

Pray out loud: "Jesus, I confess that You are my Lord and Savior. I believe in my heart that God raised You from the dead. By faith in Your Word, I receive salvation now. Thank You for saving me."

The very moment you commit your life to Jesus Christ, the truth of His Word instantly comes to pass in your spirit. Now that you're born again, there's a brand-new you!

Please contact us and let us know that you've prayed to receive Jesus as your Savior. We'd like to send you some free materials to help you on your new journey. Call our Helpline: **719-635-1111** (available 24 hours a day, seven days a week) to speak to a staff member who is here to help you understand and grow in your new relationship with the Lord.

Welcome to your new life!

Receive the Holy Spirit

As His child, your loving heavenly Father wants to give you the supernatural power you need to live a new life. *"For every one that asketh receiveth; and he that seeketh findeth; and to him that knocketh it shall be opened…how much more shall* your *heavenly Father give the Holy Spirit to them that ask him?"* (Luke 11:10–13).

All you have to do is ask, believe, and receive!

Pray this: "Father, I recognize my need for Your power to live a new life. Please fill me with Your Holy Spirit. By faith, I receive it right now. Thank You for baptizing me. Holy Spirit, You are welcome in my life."

Some syllables from a language you don't recognize will rise up from your heart to your mouth (1 Cor. 14:14). As you speak them out loud by faith, you're releasing God's power from within and building yourself up in the spirit (1 Cor. 14:4). You can do this whenever and wherever you like.

It doesn't really matter whether you felt anything or not when you prayed to receive the Lord and His Spirit. If you believed in your heart that you received, then God's Word promises you did. *"Therefore I say unto you, What things soever ye desire, when ye pray, believe that ye receive* them, *and ye shall have* them*"* (Mark 11:24). God always honors His Word—believe it!

We would like to rejoice with you and help you understand more fully what has taken place in your life!

Please contact us to let us know that you've prayed to be filled with the Holy Spirit and to request the book *The New You & the Holy Spirit*. This book will explain in more detail about the benefits of being filled with the Holy Spirit and speaking in tongues. Call our Helpline: **719-635-1111** (available 24 hours a day, seven days a week).

Call for Prayer

If you need prayer for any reason, you can call our Helpline, 24 hours a day, seven days a week at **719-635-1111**. A trained prayer minister will answer your call and pray with you.

Every day, we receive testimonies of healings and other miracles from our Helpline, and we are ministering God's nearly-too-good-to-be-true message of the Gospel to more people than ever. So, I encourage you to call today!

Endnotes

1. *Strong's Definitions*, s.v. "ἀγωνίζομαι" ("agōnizomai"), accessed July 6, 2023, https://www.blueletterbible.org/lexicon/g75/kjv/tr/0-1/.

2. Marie Barnett, "This Is the Air I Breathe," Mercy/Vineyard Publishing, 1995.

3. *American Dictionary of the English Language (Webster's 1828 Dictionary)*, s.v. "desperate," accessed June 27, 2023, https://webstersdictionary1828.com/Dictionary/desperate.

4. *Blue Letter Bible*, s.v. "σῴζω" ("sōzō"), accessed July 5, 2023, https://www.blueletterbible.org/lexicon/g4982/kjv/tr/0-1/.

5. *American Dictionary of the English Language (Webster's 1828 Dictionary)*, s.v. "grace," accessed July 6, 2023, https://webstersdictionary1828.com/Dictionary/grace.

6. Trisha R. Peach, "Burnout, Timeout, and Fallout: A Qualitative Study of Why Pastors Leave Ministry," (Doctoral thesis, Bethel University, 2022), 7, 49-50, and 134, https://spark.bethel.edu/cgi/viewcontent.cgi?article=1804&context=etd.

7. James Dobson, "Pastors and Churches Are Struggling," *Apostolic Information Service*, Dec. 20, 2007, https://www.apostolic.edu/pastors-and-churches-are-struggling/.

8. *American Heritage Dictionary of the English Language*, s.v. "acknowledge," accessed June 28, 2023, https://ahdictionary.com/word/search.html?q=acknowledge.

About the Author

Andrew Wommack's life was forever changed the moment he encountered the supernatural love of God on March 23, 1968. As a renowned Bible teacher and author, Andrew has made it his mission to change the way the world sees God.

Andrew's vision is to go as far and deep with the Gospel as possible. His message goes far through the *Gospel Truth* television program, which is available to over half the world's population. The message goes deep through discipleship at Charis Bible College, headquartered in Woodland Park, Colorado. Founded in 1994, Charis has campuses across the United States and around the globe.

Andrew also has an extensive library of teaching materials in print, audio, and video. More than 200,000 hours of free teachings can be accessed at **awmi.net**.

Contact Information

Andrew Wommack Ministries, Inc.
PO Box 3333
Colorado Springs, CO 80934-3333
info@awmi.net
awmi.net

Helpline: 719-635-1111 (available 24/7)

Charis Bible College
info@charisbiblecollege.org
844-360-9577
CharisBibleCollege.org

For a complete list of our offices, visit **awmi.net/contact-us.**

Connect with us on social media.